SOFT WATER

Charles Scott

MADHAT PRESS
ASHEVILLE, NORTH CAROLINA

MadHat Press
MadHat Incorporated
PO Box 8364, Asheville, NC 28814

The Library of Congress has assigned
this edition a Control Number of
2016909256

ISBN 978-1-941196-33-5 (paperback)

Text by Charles Scott
Cover design by Marc Vincenz

www.MadHat-Press.com

First Printing

SOFT WATER

For Dr. MacRae,
— One of the Good Guys.
Wish we would have met
under different circumstances.
Hope you find something
to like —

All Best,
Charles Scott

Preface

What isn't spoken is at the heart of Charles Scott's work. Especially when writing about Vietnam, reticence makes the poems more disturbing and more moving than if they had tried to overwhelm us. Their restraint is like the moment before something happens. And then the silence of aftermath feels like a tribute to the lost. Consider the first stanza of "All Day in Quang Nam Province":

> Early in the morning
> when it was cool and damp
> and the mist moved up
> from the river,
> and dippers were in the water
> already feeding
> and flapping their dirty wings,
> John took an AK round
> in the head
> over the right ear—
> not deep—
> and his face
> went limp and soft
> and his voice kept repeating
> "Fucking Jesus"
> "Fucking Jesus"
> in dark red letters.

It's as if the poet were saying, "This is the way it was that day, and many other days as well, but on that particular morning John took an AK round in the head. What else should I tell you except his name, and what he said?" In the poem image surrounds event— the mist moving up from the river, the dippers in the water, then what occurred, then those "dark red letters." And at the end of the poem: evening, a shrine by the river, voices singing. That they all seem in some way equal is the terror the poem knows too well and refuses to insist upon. A man dies. An apparently calm voice speaks of what otherwise could not be said without breaking down. This, the poem suggests, is how some of us survive.

But war is only part of the world of *Soft Water*. This is also a book about love, and family, and the perilous balances of the everyday. Now, with a wife and a son, "Most days/I'm fine," the poet says. He plays with his child who holds a dinosaur in each hand. "... we spin/and spin. Yesterday/I was dancing./Today/I'll dance again." Outside, the world flourishes: "millet, milo-maize; fat/meadows thick with vetch, lespedeza,/fescue, and alfalfa ..."

But even Scott's nature poems, full of those wonderful names, feel elegiac:

> ... last night I listened to the wind
> and heard the sound of air
> rushing
> through the slender, prickly stalks
> making them cry like babies
> keening in the night
> through the shadows of the garden—
> all gone
> to chokecherries, hackberries, jimsonweed.

I've known Charles Scott's poems for a long time, and they haunt me. They're beautiful and unnerving, often at the same moment. In one the poet wakes from a dream feeling "too much/has been wasted, stolen, given away." But the poems exist, poised against all this loss. They save what they can save.

—*Lawrence Raab*

For Janice and Jesse,

and for Lawrence Raab, mentor and friend

Table of Contents

For old, unhappy, far-off things,
And battles long ago;
                    —Wordsworth

The beauty that shimmers
in the yellow afternoons of October,
who ever could clutch it?
                    —Emerson

YOU'VE LEFT EVERYTHING OUT

Put it in
about the row upon row
of corncob jelly, the neatly tied packages
of snapping-turtle meat, the two gray geese
that hog the yard and dog the footsteps
of the mailman, the highchairs and handcuffs
and ball-peen hammers,
the women standing in the road
watching their bonnets
blow away forever.
Don't forget the war,
but for romance
give the weapon a handle
of coca bola wood instead of plastic.
Put in the Portuguese girl
who purely loved
what her body did to men, the speckled
Dominicker chickens
bathing in the dust beside the door.
Put in the woman with gray hair flowing
digging in the tulips, the ravens feasting
around the stupid fat cows who drop their calves
too early in the sleet before the spring,
the pelican and the scorpion and the floating bloated seals
in Ensenada harbor. Suggest
preemptive mourning
for losses yet to come, but put
someone nice at home waiting. Tell her
about the baggy cartoon pants
and the hug-me-tight jacket

1

woven from the coarse outer hair of blue sheep
on the Isle of Skye, and,
stripey-gray fur or no,
mention
this old cat
asleep in the flower bed
wild with red geraniums
and camomile.

ALL DAY IN QUANG NAM PROVINCE

Early in the morning
when it was cool and damp
and the mist moved up
from the river,
and dippers were in the water
already feeding
and flapping their dirty wings,
John took an AK round
in the head
over the right ear—
not deep—
and his face
went limp and soft
and his voice kept repeating
"Fucking Jesus"
"Fucking Jesus"
in dark red letters.

All afternoon
on full alert,
exchanging fire, surrounded,
outnumbered, everyone
thinking *overrun*, we pounded
the hills
with high explosives,
napalmed
up and down
the tree line, until
three regiments
vanished in the smoke.

In the evening
the shrine by the river
was the last thing visible.
In the clouds of incense
that drifted up the hill
through coils of concertina wire
stretched over ancient headstones
I heard voices singing,
whispering—
Grackle, black bird
with yellow bill,
to live forever
is to lose nothing,
to lose nothing
is to die.

Load of Ice near An Loc

Some men were killed on the ice run
from Da Nang back out to Finger Five
on the river overlooking Ambush Alley during Tet.

Staff Sergeant Jackson had traded
a pile of captured weapons
for twenty cases of beer.
Everyone was tired of warm beer, which meant
someone had to take a truck and make a run
to the Ice Plant in Da Nang.

The Captain wanted a corporal, he wanted me.
I argued with Sergeant Jackson,
but there has always got to be a
senior "NCO in charge."
That was the whole problem.
I didn't want to be in charge, to be responsible
for any more men.
I had already decided, by then,
that if I made it through the war,
I was never again going to be in charge
of anything.

But the Captain wanted a corporal, and I went
into Da Nang. We left early, made several other stops,
then picked up the ice and started back
in the middle of the afternoon.
I didn't make any mistakes,
I knew they were out there,
the Doc Lap Battalion.

But they were quick and clean and gone
before the pieces
stopped falling.
After everything had settled, it was quiet
because there were no wounded,
everyone that was hurt
was dead.

The muddy truck with yellow letters
filled with ice and men
came to rest upside down
at the foot of a dike
just this side of An Loc.
Some of us had once again
escaped without a scratch.

It became necessary
to arrange the dead.
Casualties were moderate to heavy.
Under the remains of the truck
was one of them
with no head,
but on each outstretched wrist
there was a watch.
I had watched him steal the second watch
at China Beach only hours before.
I remember wondering why.
Even without a head, this one was an easy
positive I.D. for me,
as I had known him for two years.

This one, under the truck, was no one
special. This was plain Bob Schumacher
small-time watch thief.

After help arrived, I didn't help.
I sat and smoked and watched
the two retrieval teams go about their work.
"Fire teams out and watch the tree line!"
The dead, with all their essential parts,
were systematically bagged to be sent off
to Graves Registration.
The load of ice, to the least recognizable shard,
was salvaged from the muck
to be sent on to the compound.
Sometimes the dead were in the way
and lay half-sprawled over a valuable
chunk of ice.
They were moved, of course—
The sergeant in charge of the clean-up crew
called it "Prioritizing the remnants."

There was one survivor, though,
who didn't like the way
things were being done.
He was crying,
and he gave a speech of sorts
while standing knee-deep in the water
at the edge of the paddy,
a large, black marine
with tears running down his cheeks,

who shouted into the dead center
of the small talk:
"A little respect for the dead,
Fuckheads.
These sacks of shit were *people*,
your people,
and they *ain't* comin' back!"

And I, at least,
felt properly rebuked.

Below Garrison Dam: 1969

I spent ten days with Clay
in Washburn, North Dakota.
The wheat was turning yellow,
it was hot, there was
nothing much to do.

One old riverboat, the *Yellow Wolf*,
sat high and dry
in sand and weeds
on the banks of the Missouri.
We climbed aboard.

We didn't talk
about the war, or
how he lost his leg
in the gardens
along the Perfume River,

and I got mine
in July, didn't mention Operation
Allen Brook—how we went
against elements
of the 308th NVA Division,

how the engineers
finally rigged a shower—
6x6 beams topped by a large steel drum—
out on the edge of the compound
against the wire,

9

a long walk in skivvies, boots,
and flak jacket, even with
a loaded rifle. Sometimes snipers
loosed a round just to see us
flop in the mud.

Once they managed to slip
through the wire, place
a mine under the mud—
it made a mess of Lance Corporal Johnson,
took his leg off at the knee.

We didn't talk about
any of that. We
watched the sun go down
and up and down again, had
whiskey in our water.

Sometimes carloads of girls
would come and sun
on gaudy towels. Although he
had dated some
before the war,

they kept their distance. Once
the one that was his cousin
waved.
On the third day
she brought

a quart of Windsor and a lunch,
left them on the deck
while we slept on the roof
of the cabin. We moved
as little as possible—

as if waiting for
something
to tell us
where to go, how to get there,
what to do when we did.

We were glad
we still had
something to shoot
for. No one wants to realize
nothing,

no one,
will ever come
to change you
into more
than a survivor.

Charles Scott

BEAR

I was patient,
living high on the mountain
on grouseberries, bannock,
and cutthroat trout,
high on the mountain
where I hid
for one full circle
of the seasons.

After the war I wanted more
elbow room and fewer people.
It was perfect for that.
There was nothing
up there. Only
the cinnamon bear.
She reared up and hooted
the first day she saw me
sitting in the doorway of the cabin,
as if she knew the whole story,
as if she thought it funny—
me living there
beneath the fire-killed larch.

We became friends,
but I knew
with *my* luck …
and that's the way it happened.
She didn't make it,
got in trouble killing stock
down on the ranch.

One hot day a trapper
blew her brains out in a thicket.
I heard the shots
and happened on them. He
leaned against a tree,
smoked his pipe and swatted flies
while his Cree wife
straddled the thing
that used to be a bear.
With a slim-bladed knife
she slipped
the hide from the carcass.

Because of the heat—
this is the way it's done—
there had to be a distribution
all up and down the valley.
Everyone was obliged
to gorge themselves
to keep the meat from going off.

In the smoky cabin
I kept the fire of jack pine
burning.
Winter passed.
When spring came again
I checked the maps,
thought things might be better
a little farther north—maybe above
the Arctic Circle. If I

could get across Eagle River,
I could go all the way
to the Beaufort Sea.

SWEDE MINE

In 1936 the Mounties carried out
Pederson the Swede
and the Finn with no name,
hauled them down
stiff across the saddle
limbs crashing through the brush
beside the trail. Now scrap
fills the meadow:
rusted coffee pot, busted shovel,
portable forge, longboard skis.
The only ghosts here are old
and not mine,

though once they woke me
in the middle of the night
trying with all their might
to push over the tall tamarack snag
I slept beneath. Woke me
from a sound sleep
like the war, like the flat smack
of rockets coming in. So many ways
to get wounded in your sleep.
A hundred feet up—in clean still air—
the tip swayed back and forth
but wouldn't snap.

I've brought others here. Everyone
whispers, no one
wants to spend the night
even though it means

15

scrambling down the scree
in the dark. Another
beautiful place
with a history of its own, where all
you can be is a stranger.
I made the climb one last time
to say goodbye. I'll miss
the calm. Up here,

high in the horseshoe basin,
whiskey jacks fly beneath the cliffs
and mosquitoes rise
from under crusted clumps of snow,
but summer never really comes
to the headwaters of the Weaselhead.
Beyond the cabin's crumbling walls
last year's half-gnawed goat bones
lie strewn around the firepit's fallen rocks,
scattered among alpine flowers so delicate
it takes them twenty-seven years to recover
from a footstep.

Old Ordnance

In March of '68
we moved into a new
compound, a drained paddy
bulldozed and doctored
so nothing would grow
to interfere
with lines of fire.

Our tent was pitched
next to a smoking hole—6 foot
by 10 foot, 4
feet deep—filled
with old ordnance: mortar
rounds, claymores, rockets,
even HE rounds
for the Army's
two long needle-nose
one-seven-fives in Da Nang.

For two days
the smoke increased. It was a mess
I expected
to start cooking off
any time. No one else
seemed concerned. Sgt. Sewell said,
"So what." I spoke
to the Lieutenant
and the Captain, complained
until the engineers
down the road

came to check it out.
Touching nothing, they
filled it over
with dirt, then
sped away in a green jeep
that flew the Rebel flag—vanished
into their own dust,
laughing,
whistling,
singing
"People Get Ready."

In 1993
when death appears
in my dreams,
it appears like that—
dull gleam
of metal
wreathed and wrapped
in drifting tendrils
of pungent smoke—Curtis Mayfield
and the Impressions
singing sweetly
in the background.

Sand Dollar Island

Something about fingering
the velvety wings of a bat,
when the alarm goes off. I
fumble for the clock, click
the button, lift its face
close to mine. The little hand
and the big hand appear
in bluey luminescence—4:30.

You wouldn't think
the war would be a factor
on a day like this
in 1991. This is the outing day
on the bay at Beverly, Massachusetts,
canceled once already
because of the fierce squall that blew up
the picnic, sent us huddled to the bandstand. We
looked out at the abandoned,
hastily covered dishes, remarked
on the angry angle
of the rain.

But today we'll boat
up and down the bay,
skewing sluggishly, towing
one or two behind on the tube.
We'll idle across the bar
to the island,
hover
over one foot of water,

19

through which sand dollars
shine like coins—
bright Spanish doubloons—strewn
on the muddy bottom.

Nearly everyone will be
in the water, the white and bronze ladies
uncomfortable in their suits, exposing more
than they would like. They'll be wading
stiff-legged, like hens, each surrounded
by her own flock of children,
searching for souvenirs. Even
our pale friend, Richard, from L.A.
will appear
sleek in the water, all
streamlined down to hollows
and essence
from the cancer.

These are my friends, but I
won't go in, will only watch
as they frolic around me.
I know how it will be—as if this
is not my life. I'll bare
my upper body, but nothing more.
They'll think it's because I can't swim
that I'm afraid; they'll try
to reassure me.
Around the bay the widows' walks
will all be empty, as no one

waits for anyone to come home.
At turn of tide we'll be
safely back in the boat heading in,
and once again nothing
will have been revealed.

Charles Scott

Dogs

Tie up all the howling dogs
Lance and Major,
Bubba and Tony,
the long-ribbed and hungry hounds.
No one's coming home from the war.

No hunting
along the frozen river.
No cedar fires.
Silent,
the bell-like voices
of the trackers.

No haloed yellow moon.
No snapping frost.
No smoke

from the chimney
slinking away along the ground
like a whipped cur.

Tie up all the howling dogs.
It's over.

I Keep Having the Same Dream, Nearly Pastoral

She sits with her hair down
in the summer kitchen by the garden.
In lamplight it shines
blue as a blackbird
against the white nightgown
with rickrack on the bodice. Night bugs

tap against the screens. Outside:
snap beans and limas, the sheepdog
grumbling in his sleep, the high
excitement of hollyhocks
pressed against the fence. We walk

through joe-pye weed and horse balm
near the river. A whickering
pinto pony
runs lambent-limbed and lovely
in the dusk.

We never speak, but sometimes
the distance between us
shimmers
like a rock-struck streetlight
that flares

into a burst of brightness
before it shatters,
and I wake up feeling too much
has been wasted, stolen, given away.

Almost grateful
for such specific sadness,
I lie in the dark and replay
the final image, hoping maybe next time
she'll remember

how I loved her yellow dress—floating
around her—gliding
through the high summer grass,
as lush and green
as the life stretched out before us
neither could believe.

SLEEPING PORCH

If I had a sleeping porch, of course
I'd get better. A sleeping porch
can dissolve and cure
the hardest kernel of hurt.
Let it be attached
to a sun-parched long-unpainted house
almost lost
back in the hills. Two rooms
and a lean-to would suffice—no
electricity, and no neighbors,
of course. I'd paint the floor
lemon yellow, to backlight
blue-tailed lizards
pumping in the sun—yellow
is the only color
that doesn't remember death.

I'd wake
to the liquid notes of blackbirds
and cardinals
dueting in the pine.
Along the river, someone
would be running hounds.
I'd love the way
they'd hit the blue note
in their baying. An old dog fox
would trot up the hill, staying
just ahead of the pack.
Headed for the thick brush
on the ridge, he'd lope

Charles Scott

across the garden, disappear
into the trees.

Every evening, from the clumped grasses
of the pasture, goatsuckers
would bring me luck, and when
the two black mules—fat
and prime—chased bullheads
in the shallows of the pond, it
would look like dancing. All night,
in my dreams—convalescing under stars
as thick as snakes in the canebrake,
over the sighing
of the wind—I'd be aware
of the heart's fluttering wingbeats,
like sparrows
helicoptering up to the feeder,
getting stronger
every day.

Blue

The sky
when it keeps
a proper distance;
some water; fur
on my Russian
Blue tomcat
who thrashed around
and died; really
open eyes; bad days
and nights; the shirt
for the yellow paisley tie;
and truth—too crude
to be attractive,
but it's blue
as your favorite
flowered wrapper
or the weathered trim
on that sprawling summer house
high in the Gatineau Hills;
robin's eggs; blossoms
of the indestructible
weeds on the lawn;
and oh, the ecstasy
within despair, deep
but also blue,
as blue as the rats of God,
their skittering claws,
their slender shining tongues.

HOCUS-POCUS

Now there's only one bar left in town
with a stuffed bobcat, and the high school
has gone to seven-man football.
I don't know when I'll get back
to San Francisco. I'm off to Canada
when I'm finished here. The blacksmith
in Afton, Oklahoma, shoes no horses.
He brazed the broken armrest
on my banjo, was glad
to get the work. He conjured first,
burnt a rich mixture
of Dutch tobacco, kinnikinnick,
and red willow, so the joint would
be strong. You would have liked
the smell.

Do I believe
in this
hocus-pocus? Yes,
just as you
believe in yours.
When I close my eyes
I think of you
and California—how
I miss the blue canoe
bobbing on the waters of the bay,
sliding down the Russian River,
the bull carp rolling
and flashing in the sun above the riffles,

the shiny black enamel of the name
painted on the stern: *No Return.*

Maybe
it's as simple
as you suggested;
maybe you're right
that I'm always
wanting any place
that's some place else.
Today,
I sit belly-deep in Horse Creek,
a half-empty can of beer
floating at my side, full ones
resting on the bottom. Yellow perch fry
nibble at the hair
on my ankles. You'd love the way
they flick themselves and disappear.

Banjo Lesson

It's 1951. I'm three
years old, back home again
in the Ozarks.

My grandfather and I
sit on the back stoop
of my Aunt Pat's house.

My uncle's hounds
loll in their pen—he's off
to the Korea War.

The sun sinks
toward Pilot Knob
beyond the white oak,

whose trunk
is wider than the sun.
Evening.

My grandfather takes
the big wooden circle
off the banjo.

We polish
everything. I do
the circle.

He replaces it
with his tool, wipes
down the strings,

drinks wine
from a glass jug
with a little hole

for your finger.
I sip some
from my cup—it's redder

than sassafras tea. My mama
comes to the screen door
about the wine.

My grandfather says
it's OK. I say
I don't want to go

back to Texas
anymore.
A black buzzard's wing

hangs over the door.
We don't get sick.
My grandfather

picks up
the banjo
and starts to play. It sings—

deedle-deedle, deedle-deedle,
deedle-deedle, dumpling.
It sings

of trace chains, heartwood, tiny
flying squirrels.
Nobody dies.

From the Frontier

All winter, hounded
by a shaggy wind,
barbarians from the north.
This army—like the last leaf
twisting on a tree—
lingers. The General himself
has lost
three fingers to the frost.
Daily
we clear the dead
from the outer ramparts—the enemy
so close
their faces look like ours.

IF I WERE A REAL WINO

It's too easy to get lost
in the bright flowers
and dusty streets of Mazatlan
where people sleep
on roofs and sidewalks
seeking relief
from night air filled with lust
as damaging as goats in the garden
or crows
rapacious in the orchard
knocking down
what they don't eat. Silence
is a mouth filled with fruit. Oh,
to be immune
to the marrow-
sucking madness of the moon.
Yesterday, I saw a man
wrapped in bitterness
as in a cloak
clasped tightly at the throat—the style
this season
for those who are whacked-out
quietly.

⟋⟋

Sprawled
in the leaves.
Morning.
The high bridge.

The yellow dog. Brown birds
around the water.
No houses.
No traffic.
The hard sun
splintering the branches
of a tree. Crawl
the tall bank
to the road.
That uneasy, queasy
hunch in the gut: maybe
Mississippi?

In Ottawa people lunch
along the Rideau Canal
all summer. Bicycles.
Ducks. The sharp towers
and steep roofs
of Parliament Hill. I lean
my head against the wall. How cool
it is this morning,
as if summer
will really end.
The goddamned birds
keep singing: *You are old,*
Father Time.

If I were a sure-enough real
wino, I'd tell them
the truth
about the Sixties, how scary
elephant grass
is. I'd say
the flamethrower
is a simple machine
that works
off kitchen matches
and jellied gasoline.

I'd tell them
waking up alive
is not the same
as being blown
into two pieces
while you sleep
and still retaining
the gift of speech,
like Jim from Texas.
I'd have them
fence me in again
with barbed wire
and make me safe.

Who could forget
the engineers
with their gaunt German shepherds,
who lived in ammo-box dugouts

in the mud along the river,
who lived like animals
passing in and out
through their tattered
and flapping burlap doors. Pohl
was from Idaho, McKay
from Colorado.

If I were a sure-enough real
wino, right now I'd be
outside the mall
stepping back and forth
in unison like the Pips,
singing: "The earth is just
a spinning ball
where all
of us are buried,"
or something
we could drink to.

Just Now the Breeze

Just now the breeze
lightly stirs,
slightly lifts the leaves
of the gray-bark willow.
On the railing
daddy longlegs
dances in place, long
second set of legs
seeking
something familiar
to believe in,
the other six
merely marking time.

SNOW SNAKES

I was born
in my grandfather's house
on the banks
of the Little Niangua River.
The girl next door, who babysat,
used my suspenders as a leash.
I pleaded, "Don't hold me no more."
She didn't listen. Still,
I grew rapidly. I thrived.

The whole place
was lousy with snakes. Blacksnakes
dangled from the rafters
of the barn. Timber
rattlers hid
on the dry sidehill
beneath the pines. Once
in the ditch
beside the mail box, a cluster
of baby moccasins, delicate
as the fingers of a child.

From the woodpile, a copperhead
struck viciously,
repeatedly,
at my mother
the morning I was born. She turned
his skin into a belt.

After so many years
away, home
is where a man in a bar
pulls a gun on you
because he doesn't remember
who you are
and doesn't like your looks.

Houses are empty now
all through these hills.
Last week the floor
of the Reed place collapsed
into the cellar, cookstove
and all. Frost

has finally taken the leaves
of the Nanking cherry, turned
the last few
black as bombazine. The graveyard's
fluttering celebration
of feather charms on sticks
rises
from a skift of snow.

Snow snake season
imminent. No longer
just a joke to explain
the jug of snake-bite medicine
behind the stove. Truly
they are there,

cruel and hammer-headed,
venomous, lithe, and pale,
undulant
beneath the glitter,
covered over,
blending in.

LAST NIGHT IN THE WIND

I couldn't sleep,
kept seeing your face—
head thrown back, neck
stretched into a slender
fluted column, then saw
you sleeping on your side, legs
tangled in the sheets.

I went down and raked
a stick across the ribs
of the culvert, listened
to the echoes. The past
was just an irritation,
like burs from vacant lots
clinging to my socks.

The moon was yellow
through the branches of the pine.
Did you know
it would happen like this, this need
necessary as the row
of poplars, rooted in the wind,
but restless on the crest of the hill?

Postcard from Nebraska

There's road work this summer
all over Nebraska. I know
you know how it feels—like
some crew's come through
with heavy equipment. Garbage
bags catch on barbed-wire fences.
They flap in the mirror
like memories—black
nighties
fluttering with lust.
Three days driving, road brain
for a week. I drove all day
singing: *Love, if you love me,*
buy me a piano-playing chicken
like the one I saw in Omaha.
The wind keeps roaring
hot from the south. Outside
the Super 8 Motel
in Broken Bow, Nebraska, right now
it's sweeping through the trees
over the happiness
of people drinking whiskey,
singing, frying fish.
The couple across the street sleeps
with windows open. The woman cries
like a sea gull when she comes.
You were right, I was wrong,
we could never
live here—nothing
but rolling humps of buffalo grass

47

and scattered clumps of willow, maybe
once a day, tiny dots
of something moving miles away—far
too open for me. I keep thinking
Delaware and Wisconsin, the only
states I haven't seen. Plus
I'd like to take another look
at Holly Springs, Mississippi.
Just driving through
it felt like home.

My Mother's Hair

When I was little, I used to like
to brush my mother's hair,
black and glossy.
I'd sit on the back of the sofa
and brush until, sometimes,
she fell asleep. Other times
we talked, and once she told me
what she'd told her father—something big,
I forget, that she wanted to do. I stopped, dropped
the brush and listened.

Just one of those times when talk—when words
are better than touching, better than anything
we know.
Better than sex. The mind
lopes along behind
following the trail, casts about
for the hottest track: No,
no, no, then suddenly—Yes!
And yes.

Charles Scott

FIREBUGS ALONG THE RIVER

Yesterday, the sun shattered
the surface of the lake, while millet ripened
in small patches
under a concentration of birds.
Red wasps were sluggish, uncertain
of the weather. All day
it threatened rain. In the evening
I watched
firebugs along the river
and those pickup trucks full of cane cutters
rattling over the dusty road
going home
steering by the sliver of the moon.

All night my dreams
disturbed me. Early, I heard
the swooping cries of a great crane
lost in the morning mist. First light,
the cedar waxwing sings
in the chinkapin tree beside the porch. I play
the pale yellow ocarina—light notes
that float out
over the okra in the garden.

The radio plays the same
sad song about some guy, rain. The announcer
wishes me good morning
but doesn't really mean it, then talks
about small bright things, and life,
that "radiant confusion." Some politician

comes on and says, "Accept it. This
is the world we live in."

I'm waiting
for some different news. Yellowhammers
feed here often. I think of them
as messengers of sorts—it's
an ornithological Morse code
I'm learning to unravel. Let
them be yellowhammers of significance, sent
from another world, one
that doesn't squeak like a young rabbit
clamped
in the jaws of a cat—that
other world
decently wet
with expectation, a world we'll enter
without hesitation and find
a way to love.

WHAT I WANT

is to write a poem
not about the war.
I want to go back
to the pale, washed-out sun
of 1951. I want
to eat a grilled-cheese sandwich
in Lone Pine, California,
with custard for dessert and hear
"Walkin' My Baby Back Home"
on the radio. I'll drink
all my milk.

I like to think, here in Calgary
—right now—
in one of those little houses
built in the boom of 1910,
an old man is sitting
before a small fire,
looking out the window
at the Elbow River
and thinking, "It's a
lovely winter's day."

And me?
I just want
to go around
knocking on doors.
I want to say
"Hello, it's me."

Red Weather

This evening, no clouds—
just dissipating vapor trails from jets
and far below some swallows.

The '52 Hudson Commodore
crouches in jimsonweed and cockleburs
beside the fallen barn.

The sun's low-angled rays
shoot blue needles of light
from the chrome of the bumper,

as another suicide
slashes through the air
from the bridge in Pasadena.

Everything trembles
until night
comes slamming down.

Once again—for the third year—
no fluttering painted ladies
swarm the lilac bush,

though inchworms on the catalpa
still measure the difficult distance
of the day.

THE GARDEN

This morning, once again,
the world is awash
with blackbirds, though winter
lingers on—hundreds
of tiny airplane imprints
decorate
last night's dusting
of snow—soon
tall and hardy thistles,
cleverly disguised
as delphiniums,
will rise in the garden.

Three blue jays
bob up and down,
singing and sounding
like a chorus of cockatoos
being eviscerated
in the lone locust tree
that defies
the classic silhouette—its branches
growing every which way,
while the woods are still
nothing more
than gray sticks
against a brittle sky.

VETERANS

Today they're scattered
over the roof garden.
Some alone,

others, like doves
or pigeons perched in pairs
on the cactus-tiered terrace,

comparing hair loss
and scars.
Mostly they don't want

to die. They complain
the food's inedible, talk
about how sad it is

these days; you can't
smoke in bed
or even in the building.

Just passing through
Pennsylvania,
for two days

I stop
to visit Pete,
who came home

Charles Scott

from a second tour
and wrapped his head
around a tree.

The first night he said,
"I was walking down the street
twenty years after

on a warm spring day,
thinking of nothing.
I saw a ball-point pen

lying on the sidewalk,
bent over, reached
to pick it up,

then jumped
like I was hit
by 20,000 volts

when a voice whispered:
Watch out,
it might be wired.

I picked it up anyway,"
he said, "stood up
and looked around,

wanted to make sure
no one noticed me
thinking like a damn fool."

The last morning, before
we said goodbye,
I wheeled him

and all his equipment
to the roof, then left him
smoking in the jungle

of pampas grass,
bamboo,
and ornamental trees.

I kept thinking
about the night
he got drunk and crazy,

stole the coordinates
for the nearest ville
from Foxtrot Battery CP.

It took three of us
to hold him down.
He wanted

simply
to blow them all away
and go home.

The Sound of Air

It's early. Coffee's
nearly ready. These days
I'm no good
until I've had a second cup.
Out the kitchen window there is nothing
but hickory-covered hills
and somebody's redbone hound
working through the brush
along the creek. There's
the spotted Poland China sow
trotting from the trees, carrying sticks
to the hog house.
Weather's coming.

These are the days of fall
and disorder. I always thought
when I got older things would change.
Even the past would alter,
as if in memory all things
could be more flexible,
as if there really had
been a choice.

But then,
last night I listened to the wind
and heard the sound of air
rushing
through the slender, prickly stalks
making them cry like babies
keening in the night

through the shadows of the garden—
all gone
to chokecherries, hackberries, jimsonweed.

All over Kansas

Wearing silk socks
with tiny patterns
of diamonds
and stars,
my great-grandfather sat
through the heat of summer
bundled up
on a couch in a darkened room.
Under wedding pictures
of his father
and his father's father,
he looked straight ahead
over a bushy white moustache.
I was eleven, in his room
with him when he died
in a bed he built himself.

That night I couldn't sleep,
kept listening to his watch
ticking in my hand.
The house was filled
with food. Outside,
on the steps his eldest son
sat up all night
with the porch light on.
Over and over
came the sound
of "Moonglow"
played slowly
and softly

Charles Scott

on a steel clarinet
while June bugs
banged against the door.

Shining in the moonlight,
cars from seven states
were parked
up against the row
of Osage orange trees,
whose fruit
dropping ripe in the night
sounded like body blows
intended to do great harm.
In the morning—all
over Kansas—sunflowers
on their long stalks
were facing east,
like my tall
cactus on the fridge, bending
toward the light.

Even at the exact
moment of his death
I was gone, already
somewhere else, wondering
Who'll feed the cats now?
and thinking about descriptions
of death
I'd read in books,
wondering why

they called it
a death *rattle*,
when it was really more
of a *rustle*,
like the wind's
sighing flutter
through dry corn.

SECOND PHASE

My wife's father
is ninety. First a year
in Assisted Living, now
nursing home
for two.
Parkinson's disease.
Dementia.

When he can,
he likes to take
his walker
up and down the hall, bother
the other residents,
go into their rooms,
stir them up.

The blind woman next door
screams from her wheelchair,
lashes out
with her stick.
It's as if
he were a small boy again—
Regina, back in the Roaring Twenties—
wandering around at night
with his chums,
tipping toilets.

He's angry
with his dead wife,
who visits every day.

She gambles now
and smokes,
dances with the staff,
though she refuses
to talk to him,
won't give him any money.

My wife tells him,
"Mom's dead, Dad. She can't.
You remember. It was
so cold
you had to stay in the limo
at the graveside.
Mom's in heaven."

"Yeah, I know," he says,
"but this is phase two.
She's running wild,
having lots of fun,
talks and laughs
with all the others.
Even if it's just
hallucination,
it's not right.
Why won't she talk to me?"

Charles Scott

THE MIND TRIES

Here I sit
sucking
on a bottle of sneaky pete:
the clattering
of leaves along the walk;
the evening air
flickering with bats; the moon,
that cheap hypnotist,
eyeing me solidly
the way an owl will stare you down
while the mind tries
to wriggle free.

I'm thinking
about the rank green wheel
of French cheese
I couldn't swallow
so whipped through the trees;
this scaling
water tower; that dummy
cannon there,
dedicated
to the GAR;

and that evening
when all the cats of Athens
swarmed the tables
of the outdoor café. Blue flies,
drowning in the dregs
of turpentine wine,

were buzzing in the bottles
—amplified and echoey
as a chorus of angels
singing in the shower—
as the lime trees
with their blossoms
one by one
blinked out.
Around the islands, the sea
was blue enough.

Charles Scott

CALIFORNIA

This time of year,
in the mountains
outside San Francisco,
banana slugs
appear—slime trails
everywhere.
Here in L.A.,
on Jackson Street,
under jacaranda trees
blooming in clouds
of purple smoke,
snails swarm
the calla lilies.

After the violence
of yesterday's rain,
the yellow blossoms
of the tall climbing rose
are splattered and blown
against the stuccoed wall.
Mockingbirds are nesting
again
in the holly-leaf cherry.
This morning, the rooster
dive-bombed
the fat, old tom
from the fence.
They don't want us here.

In Another Country

1.

When Falstaff stabs
Hotspur's corpse,
the class responds
with indignation
and revulsion.

What's the harm, really?
I want to say. I mean
he's already dead.
And what about the cannibals?
They ate

the enemy dead.
Or the mad Cherokees—Doublehead,
Pumpkin Boy, and Bench—
who broiled strips of flesh,
and the hearts and brains,

from Captain Overall
and his Indian
fighter friend
Burnett
and ate them.

2.

And what about
Vietnam?
the mutilation of the dead

by both sides—each
in an attempt

to outfreak the other,
which must have led
to some odd
and ugly prayers:
"Oh Lord, let them think

we're so crazy, they won't
fuck with us."
The class is right,
some things
are just plain wrong,

like the sniper bragging
about his three
confirmed kills—all head shots
on farmers
working in their fields.

3.
My life
these days—far
from the war,
in another country—

is daily and domestic: swingset,
sandbox, garden, cat,

the angle
of the sun on the lawn.

My son and I
pull rhubarb, pick saskatoons,
listen to the leaves rattle
on the copper beech.

At five,
he speaks English
with a Canadian accent
that sounds like home.

4.
Two boys—about
my son's age—
once lived
in a tiny hamlet near Dai Lahn.

Wearing Marine Corps caps,
every day they played
along the road
outside the compound,

smiling and chattering
at patrols
going out
or coming in,

Charles Scott

always ready
to pose
for the camera,
rolling on the ground

and hugging each other
when they made a joke.
One day, they hit a tripwire
on the trail

and disappeared.
Somewhere in a box
I have a photograph
I should have thrown away.

After the Storm

Today I'm going
to the Seniors' Center
for Tea and Conversation—
every Tuesday afternoon
from one till three, but
I remember passion
and all of that, the way you
breathed into me, your lips
on mine, flickery
as a nuthatch.

Memory touches me
more each day, like
a wand of willow, like
the whiskers of a cat,
like a hard slap.

Of course, I remember
the night we parked
the '53 Ford
beside the pond
and left
the engine running, kept
the radio
and heater on—six-volt
dash lights
turned down
to soft romantic glow,

the feel
of pebblecloth upholstery
scraping against my skin.

And the day we spent
locked up
in the cabin by the lake
during the sudden
summer storm—
how the birches swayed and shivered,
flustered by the wind.

Delicate Things

I want that which is not in this world.
—Zinaida Gippius

Even though you wear
your winter coat
and snowflakes
in your hair,
underneath
I know
you wear your
most delicate things.

There is no need
to remove them.
It doesn't matter.
Impractical things,
improbable boundaries
that your body
strains against—
there and there
and there.

Charles Scott

Garden in Alberta

A short growing season, but ...
you know, the *idea*. My two-year-old son
planted, watered, and watched.

Bugs, birds, and squirrels
wiped out half. Early frost
took the rest.

Still, we had a few glads,
and sweet peas
perfuming every room.

We'll dig it all under
and try again next year.
Across the fence now some boys

are digging in the vacant lot.
Wiser, maybe, this far north,
they're building a fort.

Each afternoon my son and I
man the porch and watch
the progress. We notice

light striking leaves, the many
shades of green. We count
and recount

the pair of magpies
patrolling the lawn.
And our garden's

just another story
my son likes
to hear me tell our guests,

like the one about
our last trip to the zoo.
Maybe he's right.

Something happens. You do this
or that. Whatever else
you get, stories

magically appear,
the way wild strawberries grow
in delicate red profusion

all over the grounds
of the old sewer plant
in North Adams, Massachusetts.

Charles Scott

THE FIFTIES

I miss the thinness
of monophonic sound,
but mostly I miss the movies
and my father, who always maintained
the Hi-Way 50 Drive-In. The last
summer of the fifties
I helped. We'd drive out early
in the red Ford pickup
and clean all day, smooth out
the go-kart track,
rehang the swings.

The last Saturday night
we got in free, I forget
the double feature, but remember
Selected Shorts: An Armistice Day tribute
to generals of the Great War.
A high-angled view of beribboned old men
snoring and twitching in the sun
against a montage
of battle scenes. The camera
like a small hungry dog
haunts the ditches
surrounding death. Disembodied voices
crying out: *Lift my head,*
give me water.

My father couldn't
pick a winner. Big-3
mechanic—Studebaker, Nash, Packard—

getting worried
by then. Dead at fifty-one
of a heart attack
in a backyard hammock
in 1964, the last year
before the war.

Over fifty now, myself,
with a son of my own, luckier
some ways—older
than he ever got to be—some days
still stuck
in the moment just before
the cars grumble back to life, flare
their headlights,
and file slowly out. The music
stops. The screen
fades to black. It feels
like all the doors of heaven
slamming in your face.

Most days
I'm fine. My son,
almost three, rides in the back
of a '54 Ford. He's never
seen a movie, won't watch
TV, but every evening
he plays his tape
of dinosaur songs. Holding a dinosaur
in each hand, we spin

and spin. Yesterday
I was dancing. Today
I'll dance again.

Like Some Stranger

Death doesn't care about you,
as you go floundering
through life
like a burro in the snow,
you with your stack of unpaid bills,
you with your squeaky brakes.

You can learn
to play the banjo and the mouth harp
and the bowl-backed mandolin,
but it will bring you no reprieve. Death
is not so easily impressed.

But death is charmed
by the way you collect gimcracks,
knick-knacks, and bric-a-brac:
your grandmother's white
linen shirtwaist
trimmed with Battenberg lace; pictures
of your grandfather's team
of fondly cherished mules; the program
from your third-grade play
about the farmer in the dell;
prom tickets; even
matchbooks
from your honeymoon hotel,

though death doesn't really
understand
your great fear

of losing them.
Death acquires nothing
that doesn't stay for good.

And one day death
will come tromping up the steps
to knock on your front door,
like some stranger
selling magazines
from a colorful brochure.

CELEBRATION

I love grouse
berry wine
sloshed around the tongue; the hard bark
of the hound; the oriole's
bright flutter; the tango and fandango
and the stately
minuet; the slippery and soft
names of rocks
the tongue loves, too: soapstone, emeralds,
moonstones, and opals;
the small exotic grains: kaffir
corn, millet, milo-maize; fat
meadows thick with vetch, lespedeza,
fescue, and alfalfa; the eyes
of doves, simply
because they're perfectly round; crows
and all those other birds
who are said to mate for life,
as if there were another reason.

LITTLE SIGNS

Every day I drive past
the old folk's home
back in the trees.
What are they looking at
with their eyes closed
propped up there on the veranda?
Things they'll never see again?
Snake doctors with crackling
cellophane wings
wheeling over the reeds?
Hickory shad, blue cats, and
alligator gar? Redhorse suckers
running wild in the shallows?
The twining
elegance of eels?

Increasingly
absent-minded
myself these days—synapses
slowing down, misfiring, slightly
out of sync. Like messages
from beyond,
they keep arriving, those
little signs
of impending doom. I begin
to understand
that look of *lost and otherwhere*
befogging the faces of the old,
surrounded as they are

by so much
unaccustomed magic.

I don't want to see
my life stretched out behind me
like a long banquet
to which no one has come, regret
approaching
sharp-nosed as a garfish
with those little
piggy eyes
and needle-like teeth,
slicing through
the murky waters of the world.
Maybe it's just another
complicated trick—all smoke
and mirrors—maybe
when the time finally comes
it will be as easy
as going to a convention
in Kansas City, or simply
lying down
with someone you love.

Charles Scott

LET IT BE

as mysterious
        as a nylon stocking
                dangling
                        from a tree

as whispery
        as snake scales
                scraping
                        across the stones

as soft
        as the skin
                on a woman's upper
                        inner thigh

as delicate
        as a deer
                sweetening its breath
                        with acorns

as brilliant
        as a muzzle flash
                bursting
                        from the trees

as graceful
        as Sonny Liston
                jumping rope
                        to "Night Train" on TV

as distinctive
        as a kingfisher's
                clicking call claiming
                        his stretch of river

as hushed
        as sleet
                sifting down
                        like sugar pouring from a sack

as persistent
        in the mind
                as a solitary word

Charles Scott

AUTUMN

Something
about the angle of the sun,
the leaves drifting down,
feels reassuring. I love it
every year when I see
the last two maple leaves
stems down and twirling.

Today, nodding along beside my wife
on the long ride back
from the hospital in the city,
I notice yellow
is beginning to appear
among the trees. Chemotherapy
and radiation.

She drives me back and forth
five days a week, paints
the sky above the meadow
over and over. Having seen
the sky so often, I sit
beside her, watching only
the squares—that

bright array
there in the tray
of the watercolor tin.

Soft Water

1.

When I bought this house
old Frank up the road
said the place was full of snakes, told me
it had been abandoned too long
to resurrect, but I know
that's not so. From the upstairs window
I can see
all the way to the tall
cottonwoods and sycamores
and the other
smaller, less distinct
trees that run to water
down on Little Moniteau Creek.

I lived here once
thirty years ago. Frank
doesn't remember. He's the same
but older
and frail. He still
sharpens scissors, knives, and saws, listens
to the sound advice of trees. On fine days
he pulls his shepherd dog up
and down the highway
in a Radio Flyer wagon. The dog
sits and smiles.

Sometimes, when Frank talks about
his war—Belleau Wood and Château-Thierry—
I think about mine, the hamlet

93

I never knew the name of, the one just past
Phu Dong, and wonder
if Calvin Lee
still has his picture—
himself sitting on a hump of dirt
surrounded by a pile
of dead marines. He is
posing with a piece
of an NVA corpse,
missing from the waist down,
sitting on his lap.
It is wearing a bloody
UC Berkeley sweatshirt—
lit cigarette
smoking from its mouth.

When I said, "Hey Calvin,
what are you going to do
with a picture like that?"
he said, "Send it to my girl."

2.

The first morning
I scrambled up the ridge
and looked into the curious eyes
of a red fox, sunning herself
on the rocks above the trail.
Sharp-nosed face resting on crossed paws, she was
unafraid.

Up there the few scattered clouds
gathered themselves
into a shape—mouth, nose, eyes—
it might have been the face
of someone looking off,
looking far.

Now the days are warmer;
things have gone to color: yellow
of forsythia, then blue flags bloom,
Scotch broom adds its softer summer yellow,
climbing roses I thought were dead
spread white petals on the porch.
My fat red hens
fluff themselves
in the dog fennel by the fence. I've settled in
for the duration.

I've cleaned the leaves, mud, and trash
from the cistern, cleaned it out
so the water's fit to use. Suppose
a woman were to
one day appear
running down
between the butternut trees
that line the lane? She'd be
hot and dusty and might
decide to stay. She'd want
soft water
to wash her hair.

... and for all those who didn't make it home ...

Acknowledgments

Cedar Hill Review: "If I Were a Real Wino"

Cimarron Review: "Hocus-Pocus"

Coal City Review: "Old Ordnance," "Bear"; the first section of "All Day in Quang Nam Province" appeared by itself as "AK."

Concho River Review: "Snow Snakes"

The Distillery: "Below Garrison Dam: 1969"

GSU Review: "Postcard from Nebraska"

The New England Intercollegiate Literary Journal: "Soft Water" and "Just Now the Breeze" appeared in slightly different form.

Nebo: A Literary Journal: "Autumn," "The Garden"

Plainsongs: "What I Want"

Plume: "From the Frontier"

Poem: "The Sound of Air," "All Over Kansas," "Celebration," "Sleeping Porch," "Firebugs Along the River"

Southern Humanities Review: "After the Storm"

Talking River Review: "You've Left Everything Out"

Trestle Creek Review: "Last Night in the Wind"

Viet Nam Generation: "Dogs"

Yalobusha Review: "I Keep Having the Same Dream, Nearly Pastoral"

Some of these poems appeared in the chapbook *Old Ordnance* (Adastra Press, 2005). The poem "Swede Mine" made its first appearance therein.

Special thanks to Marc Vincenz and everyone at MadHat Press for making this book a reality.

About the Author

CHARLES SCOTT was born in Camden County, Missouri, in 1948; he now lives in Canada. He received a B.A. from Williams College in 1993 and an M.A. from Miami University. A chapbook of his poems, *Old Ordnance*, was published by Adastra Press in 2005. Most recently his poems have appeared in *Nebo: A Literary Journal*, *Plainsongs*, *Plume*, *Poem*, and *Southern Poetry Review*. *Soft Water* is his first full-length book.

Made in the USA
Middletown, DE
12 July 2016